WORKBOOK FOR THE DOG TYPE SYSTEM FOR SUCCESS IN BUSINESS AND THE WORKPLACE

A Unique Personality System to Better Communicate and Work with Others

by Gini Graham Scott, Ph.D.
Author of *Do You Look Like Your Dog?*

WORKBOOK FOR THE DOG TYPE SYSTEM FOR SUCCESS IN BUSINESS OR THE WORKPLACE

Copyright © 2017 by Gini Graham Scott

All rights reserved. No part of this book may be used or reproduced by any means, graphic, electronic, or mechanical, including photocopying, recording, taping or by any information storage retrieval system without the written permission of the author except in the case of brief quotations embodied in critical articles and reviews.

TABLE OF CONTENTS

- INTRODUCTION 5
- CHAPTER 1: SETTING UP A WORKSHOP...7
  - Making Arrangements..7
  - Inviting Participants 7
- CHAPTER 2: INTRODUCING YOURSELF, THE WORKSHOPS, AND THE FOUR DOG TYPES 9
  - Getting Set Up..9
  - Introducing Yourself and Explaining What Will Happen 9
  - Explaining the Four Dog Type System 10
  - Are You a German Shepherd? 12
  - Are You a Pomeranian? 13
  - Are You a Golden Retriever?..14
  - Are You a Border Collie? 15
  - Rating the Dog Types...16
- CHAPTER 3: DISCUSSING THE DOG TYPE RESULTS 19
- CHAPTER 4: DESCRIBING THE ROOTS OF THE SYSTEM 21
  - The Myers-Briggs Type Indicator 21
  - The DISC Personality Profile...22
  - The Red-Blue-Yellow-Green Personality Type..22
  - How the Dog Type System Builds on What Has Gone Before 23
- CHAPTER 5: ASSESSING THE DOG TYPE OF OTHERS AND LEARNING MORE ABOUT YOUR DOG TYPE 25
  - Assessing Another Person's Dog Type...25
    - Setting Up the Exercise 25
    - Continuing the Exercise 26
    - Discussing the Exercise..26
  - Learning More about Your Dog Type 27
- CHAPTER 6: APPLYING THE DOG TYPE SYSTEM IN YOUR BUSINESS OR WORKPLACE 29
  - The Key Characteristics of the Four Types of Dogs..29
- CHAPTER 7: BETTER COMMUNICATING AND INTERACTING WITH OTHERS BASED ON THEIR DOG TYPE 31
  - Adapting Your Approach to Others 31
    - Relating to the German Shepherd (Red/Dominant Leadership Type).......................31
    - Relating to the Pomeranian (Yellow/Influencer/Fun Party Animal Type)................32
    - Relating to the Golden Retriever (Green/Steady/Cool Supporter) 32
    - Relating to the Border Collie (Blue/Conscientious/the Serious Fact Checker).........32
    - Summing Up 33

   Some Examples of Using the Dog Type System in Different Situations 33
      Making a Sale of a Product or Service.. 33
      Looking for Clients or Referrals at a Networking Event 34
      Improving Your Relationships with Co-Workers, Your Boss, or Your Employees in the Workplace 34
      Getting a Job or Promotion 36
   Conducting a Roleplay on Adapting Your Approach to Different Dog Types 37
CHAPTER 8: QUICKLY IDENTIFYING THE DIFFERENT DOG TYPES.................41
   Using the Dog Type Occupations and Orientations Chart..43
CHAPTER 9: WRAPPING UP THE WORKSHOP 47
   Summary of the Workshop 47
   Evaluating the Workshop...47
   Final Comments 49
   What's Next 49
  ABOUT THE AUTHOR 51

INTRODUCTION

This workbook is designed to accompany *Using the Dog Type System for Success in Business and the Workplace.* It provides the tools to conduct a workshop for a group of business professionals or for a team of employees in a workplace. It can be adapted for a group of any size, though it is recommended that in larger groups you divide people up into teams of 6 to 15 people, who can do these exercises together.

To lead such a group, become familiar with *Using the Dog Type System for Success in Business and the Workplace*, so you can discuss how the system works and feel comfortable asking questions on the subject. You'll find some of the topics included here, so you can give them to workshop participants as handouts. Copy those materials as indicated, in addition to the surveys, take-aways, and other materials included in this workbook.

You'll find an evaluation questionnaire for attendees to fill out to give you feedback on the workshop. You can use this information to improve your ability to lead future workshops, plus we would like copies of the responses, so we can improve the program ourselves.

There is also a workshop report form for you to copy, fill out, and send to us, so we can improve the program for everyone. We are still developing the workshop and eventually want to turn this into a certified training program. So you are on the front lines as we develop and expand the program.

This is the beginning of what we plan to develop into an international personality assessment tool to help individuals gain more success in business and the workplace. At the same time, we are developing a companion personality program for understanding oneself and others with a more expanded dog profile system. A separate workbook will be available for that, too.

We will be videotaping and creating transcripts from some workshops, and as this material is available, we will provide you with copies to help you give your own workshops.

In addition, we are developing a parallel system which works the same way, except that it features Cat Types, using the profiles of different types of cats. Books and workshops for this will be released shortly. The only difference is that you can use the Cat Type system with people who prefer using cat profiles to achieve more success in business and the workplace or to better understand oneself and others for better relationships. So once you become trained in the Dog Type system, you can easily use the Cat Type system. You just have to learn about the different cat profiles, but otherwise everything is the same.

As described at length in *Using the Dog Type System for Success in Business and the Workplace,* the four dog types selected to guide one's communication and interactions with others parallels other popular systems for self-understanding and dealing with others. These include the Myers-Briggs system based on a scale of four main categories – extraversion-introversion, feeling-thinking, perceiving-judging, and intuitive-sensing; the DISC system, based on whether one's personality is characterized by dominance, influence, steadiness, or conscientiousness; and the red, blue, yellow, and green personality type system. In this latter system, the reds are characterized as strong willed fast-thinking leaders; the yellows, as sociable, friendly, party animals; the blues, as deep-thinking analytical types, and the greens as laid-back, friendly, agreeable types, though there is some variation in assigning the yellow, blue, and green colors to different types.

To summarize, these four dog types are:

- the German Shepherd, with parallels to the person high in dominance in the DISC system or the red personality in the red, blue, yellow and green system. This might also have parallels with the extravert and thinker in the Myers-Briggs system.

- the Pomeranian, with parallels to the person high in influence in the DISC system or the yellow-personality in the red, blue, yellow and green system. They might have parallels with the extravert and feelers in the Myers-Briggs system.

- the Golden Retriever, with parallels to the person high in steadiness in the DISC system or the green personality in the red, blue, yellow, and green system. This might have parallels with the introvert and feeler in the Myers-Briggs system.

- the Border Collie, with parallels to the person high in conscientiousness in the DISC system or the blue personality in the red, blue, yellow, and green system. This might have parallels with the introvert and thinker in the Myers-Briggs system.

Conceivably, different dogs might have been chosen to represent these four classic personality types, such as selecting a Rottweiler instead of a German Shepherd; a Chihuahua instead of a Pomeranian; a Yellow Lab instead of a Golden Retriever; and a Siberian Husky instead of a Border Collie, because they share many of the same personality qualities. But the chosen dogs were selected because of their widespread popularity in the United States. As the system spreads to other countries or to certain subcultures within the U.S., other dogs might be selected

This workbook is based on using these four key types, which can be modified by each person selecting a second favorite dog. This second choice provides a fuller picture of what each person is like, since this combination of the first and second choices results in 16 personality types, though four of these are a doubling down on the first type, so that person even more strongly has that type.

The next section describes how to set up a workshop. Then, this workbook features profiles of each type of dog, followed by some guidelines for helping workshop members understand each type and chose the type they most strongly identify with. Subsequent sections provide exercises to help participants apply this knowledge in their business or workplace.

CHAPTER 1: SETTING UP A WORKSHOP

Making Arrangements

To set up a workshop, find an appropriate venue based on the size of the group. For a small group, you can use your home or a participant's home if it's large enough. Or hold the workshop in a conference room if you are doing this for a group of employees at a company. For larger meetings, check in your community for facilities you can use.

Determine a convenient time and date for the program. Generally, figure on about 2 to 3 hours, starting with 15-30 minutes to allow people to network informally, about 1 to 2 hours for the program, and another 15-30 minutes for networking after the event.

You need access to a screen where you can show off PowerPoint presentations or videos, and you have to arrange to use a projector with a hookup to your computer or a laptop, where you can insert a flash drive, CD, or DVD with the PowerPoint or video presentation. Some venues will already have a screen, projector, and computer setup, so check if that is available, or make other arrangements.

Inviting Participants

Once you have your planned venue and date, you can invite participants with an email, flyer at events you attend, or in other ways. We are developing announcement and flyer templates you can use, and will let you know when they are available. We would appreciate getting copies of any materials you develop, since we can use these for ideas to create templates for everyone. And, of course, we will recognize everyone who contributes to developing these materials.

Your invitation to this event should include the following elements, adapted to your expected participants:

- <u>an opening headline</u> that invites people to participate in a workshop that will help them in their business or work, such as:

> "You're invited to a unique workshop to become more effective in communicating with (clients/prospective customers/co-workers/people in your workplace) to gain (more clients/better relationships at work/building more effective teams)".

- <u>a brief description</u> of what this workshop is about, such as:

> "You'll discover your own Dog Type and learn how to use this technique to better understand yourself and others. This knowledge will help you better know how and when to talk to others/make pitches to get what you want/sell more products/create more interest in your service.)"

- <u>an explanation</u> for those unfamiliar with the Dog Type system, where you state that your Dog Type is the kind of dog you like most or least – or are most or least like -- whether or not you own a dog. There are four key Dog Types, which are like the four

personality types described in popular personality profile systems like Myers-Briggs, DISC, or the red-yellow-green-blue color profile.
- <u>The workshop will be held</u> (WHERE, WHEN).
- <u>Here's how to register</u> for the event (INCLUDE YOUR CONTACT INFORMATION AND REGISTRATION INFORMATION).

When people register, immediately provide them with a confirmation. Then, one week and a few days before the event, follow up by email to confirm that they are coming and welcome them to the event.

CHAPTER 2: INTRODUCING YOURSELF, THE WORKSHOPS, AND THE FOUR DOG TYPES

Getting Set Up

On the day of the workshop, arrive about a half hour early and set up the room to encourage communication and interaction. For a small group, set up chairs in a circle or have everyone sit around a conference table. For a larger group, set up smaller circles around the room or have people sit around tables.

Provide some water, coffee, snacks, and whatever else is usual for a program for business people or in a workplace in your community.

Have some nametags and pens available, so people can fill these out with their names. Bring a roster of the people who have signed up and check them in during this initial networking period. In follow-up meetings, people can include their Dog Type on their nametag in addition to their name. But in this first meeting, ask people to leave some space under their name, so they can later fill in their Dog Type.

About 5 minutes before the program starts, let people know that you plan to begin in 5 minutes.

Once it is time to begin, announce the start of the program – or if it's a large enough group, ring a loud bell. Ask people to find their seats. When everyone is seated, you can begin.

Introducing Yourself and Explaining What Will Happen

To begin the program, introduce yourself as the local coordinator and program leader. Tell everyone how glad you are to have them here and briefly introduce yourself in about 30-60 seconds. Tell others what you do and what led to your interest in leading this program.

Explain how others will benefit from this program and the Dog Type system. Adapt what you say to the type of group (ie: small businesspeople, company employees, managers and supervisors, or others). For example, some key benefits to mention are:
- better communication with others
- a more targeted way to present a pitch for sales or for yourself
- a fun way to better get to know others
- and more…

Tell everyone what you will be doing in this first program. Explain that you can lead a follow-up program if there is interest and can assist with one-on-one consulting. In particular, for this first program, explain that you will be covering:
- the four types of dogs and their profiles
- how the system was developed and was found to be effective

- how participants can apply the system in their business and workplace.
Also, participants will experience some exercises to show how this system works.
Ask people in the group if this program sounds good and pause. Normally, everyone will nod or say "okay."

Explaining the Four Dog Type System

Now it's time to introduce the Four Dog Type system. Briefly mention the four key Dog Types, which participants can use in their business or work relationships. Explain that after you briefly introduce these types, you will give a more detailed profile for each one (or, if you prefer, show this list on the screen and allow time for participants to look at the list.

You can explain the following. Use this order, which is the order commonly used in the other systems:

- <u>The German Shepherd</u>, who is the strong, aggressive leader. This person thinks quickly, wants to get to the point, and makes fast decisions.
- <u>The Pomeranian</u>, who is very lively, outgoing, and loves excitement, variety, and change. He or she is a true extravert and enjoys being the center of attention.
- <u>The Golden Retriever</u>, who is a warm, feeling, friendly person. He or she likes getting along with others, is calm and steady, and makes a good follower and team player.
- <u>The Border Collie</u>, who is thoughtful and analytical. He or she is interested in knowing the facts and takes time to review them to make a careful decision.

Then, indicate that you are giving out sheets with the four profiles, so participants can review them and keep these profiles. In order to give out the profiles, print each one on a single sheet of paper and print out enough copies, so everyone in the workshop gets a copy of the four profiles.

Let people know they will have about 5 minutes to review the profiles and think about how they are like or unlike these four types of dogs. The sheets to print up and pass out are on the following five pages.

THE FOUR DOG TYPES

The German Shepherd
　　The strong, aggressive leader. This is the person who thinks quickly, wants to get to the point, and makes fast decisions.

The Pomeranian
　　Very lively, outgoing, and loves excitement, variety, and change. He or she is a true extrovert, and enjoys being the center of attention.

The Golden Retriever
　　A warm, feeling, friendly person. He or she likes getting along with others, is calm and steady, and makes a good follower and team player.

The Border Collie
　　Thoughtful and analytical. He or she is interested in knowing the facts and taking time to reflect on and analyze them to make a careful decision.

Are You a German Shepherd?

A Little Bit of History...

If you chose a German Shepherd, you picked a dog known for its strength and courage, as well as being a popular police dog.

The German Shepherd was developed in Germany in the 1800s to herd and guard sheep. In 1899, the Verein fur Deutsche Scharferhunde SV was formed to improve the breed, so it not only made a great herding dog, but could be very courageous, athletic, and intelligent, making it an ideal police dog. It became a war sentry during WWI. For a time, its name was changed, so it wouldn't be associated with its roots in Germany, but in 1931, its original name was restored. It gained movie fame as Rin Tin Tin from the silent movie first released in 1922 and then produced as a films series and TV series, including a 1947 film with child actor Robert Blake and the 1950s TV series *The Adventures of Rin Tin Tin,* though different dogs were used over the years. It has since been a popular police dog and has helped in search and rescue operations and detecting explosives, as well as being a popular pet.

What's Your Personality and Style?

If you picked a German Shepherd, you tend to have **lots of energy**, and are very **alert, intelligent,** and **serious.** You can be **stand-offish** when you first meet someone, and tend to be **strong,** even **domineering.** You are very **protective** of those you are close to, and are very **devoted** and **faithful.** You have a strong sense of **mission** or **purpose.**

Are You a Pomeranian?

A Little Bit of History…

In case you chose a Pomeranian, this is a catlike Toy Dog, that makes a great companion.

The Pomeranians are descendants of the Nordic sled dogs and at one point they were sheep dogs before they were recognized in their diminutive form in the 1870s as a pet and show dog. It is believed they were miniaturized in Germany, particularly in Pomerania, where they got their name. Their popularity spread after Queen Victoria brought a Pomeranian home from Italy, and they were bred in her royal kennels.

What's Your Personality and Style?

If you picked a Pomeranian, you have picked a small but **feisty** toy dog, that is **very alert, vivacious, joyful,** and brimming with **high-energy.** You're also very much the **extrovert**, a real **people-person,** who loves to be with others, and makes a **warm, loving, affectionate** companion. You're usually **obedient** and **eager to please** others, and you spread your **love** and **affection** around. You love **looking good** and appreciate **good grooming,** and have a high confidence that comes with **knowing you look good**. In fact, your confidence sometimes gets you in trouble, since you're sometimes ready to challenge the "big dogs", using your **cleverness** to outwit and outplay.

Are You a Golden Retriever?

A Little Bit of History…

In case you chose a Golden Retriever, this is a sporting dogs which is among the most popular family dogs.

The Golden Retrievers were developed in Scotland and England in the early 1800s to help with retrieving game from the water as well as on land, and they came to the U.S. in the 1890s. They are especially known for their obedience, and have become popular as guide dogs for the blind, as well as good at detecting narcotics for the police, because of their sensitive smell ability.

What's Your Personality and Style?

If you picked a Golden Retriever, you tend to be a **very affectionate, warm, outgoing, extroverted people-person,** with **lots of energy**, just like these dogs. You are often **playful,** and can be very **charming,** but you're **down-to-earth,** even **humble** in your nature, not showy or ostentatious. You have an **optimistic, cheery** outlook, and are **loyal** and **devoted** to others. No wonder you are likely to be **popular** and enjoy **socializing** with others, just like these dogs.

Are You a Border Collie?

A Little Bit of History…
    If you chose a Border Collie, these are herding dogs, which are known for their helpfulness, loyalty, and obedience.
    The Border Collies trace back to the days of sheepherders, especially in Scotland, and the 18th century Scottish poet Robert Burns celebrated them as a good and faithful dog.

What's Your Personality and Style?
    If you picked a Collie or Border Collie, you have a great **get-along** personality, as someone who likes being with others. You tend to have a **gentle, mild-mannered** personality, and make a great **follower** and **team player,** because you like to **go along** with what others are doing. You are eager to **please, take directions,** and are good at **following orders.** You tend to be a **very affectionate, loyal,** and **devoted** toward those you know and trust, though you may be more **reserved** with those you don't know very well.

Rating the Dog Types

After everyone has had about 5 minutes to review the profiles, check if the participants are finished looking at them. If not, give them a few more minutes.

Once everyone is ready, ask them to <u>rate</u> the Dog Types based on how much they are most like or least like – or how much they like or don't like -- each type of dog. Explain that they should rate each dog from 1 (least like or like the least) to 10 (most like or like the most). There are two listings, and if they are the same, use that number. If they are different, take the average of the two listings.

Using this final column, they should <u>rank</u> their choices according to their score. The dog with the highest number is #1 – their Top Dog. The dog with the next highest number is #2 – their Watch Dog. The dog with the lowest number - #4 – is their Underdog. They can also consider their dog #3 their Sleuth Dog, representing a hidden strength. Should there be a tie, they should decide how to rank the dogs, so one is higher than the other.

Tell them to make these ratings and rankings as quickly as possible, so that they respond with a more intuitive or gut level reaction. They shouldn't think about the ratings – just write down their first impression in rating each dog from 1-10.

A copy of this rating sheet is on the following page. Print a copy out for each person in the workshop.

WHAT'S YOUR DOG TYPE?

Rate each of these four dogs on a scale of 1-10 based on how much you like that type of dog and how much you feel it is like you. The numbers may be the same or different. Then, combine the scores for each dog for your average score for that dog. (In other words, add the two scores together and divide by 2). Finally, rank the dogs, based on these scores – the dog with the highest score becomes #1; the next highest is #2; and so on. If there is a tie, decide which dog should be higher than the other, so that you rank the dogs from #1 to #4.

Type of Dog	**How Much Like Me**	**How Much I Like**	**Combined Score**	**Rank**
German Shepherd	_____	_____	_____	_____
Pomeranian	_____	_____	_____	_____
Golden Retriever	_____	_____	_____	_____
Border Collie	_____	_____	_____	_____

Your #1 Dog: _____ Combined Score: _____
(Your Top Dog)

Your #2 Dog: _____ Combined Score: _____
(Your Watch Dog)

Your #3 Dog: _____ Combined Score: _____
(Your Sleuth Dog)

Your #4 Dog: _____ Combined Score: _____
(Your Underdog)

CHAPTER 3: DISCUSSING THE DOG TYPE RESULTS

After everyone has filled out the Dog Type profiles, give everyone a chance to discuss them with others.

Ask everyone to get in a small group of 3 or 4 people, so they can share with each other. Encourage people to get in a group with people they don't already know. Allow about 2-2 1/2 minutes per person in a group, giving the groups about 7-10 minutes for the discussion, depending on how much time participants need.

Once everyone is in a group, give them the following instructions:
- Now talk about your choice for about 2 to 2 1/2 minutes each.
- Take turns in doing so.
- Select a person in the group to report back to the whole group on the experience.
- Whoever is reporting back should note down each person's first and last choice.
- Now in your groups, tell others what you do in your business or job and describe your first, second, and last dog choice to each other.
- Explain why you made those choices and how that is reflected in what you do in business or in the workplace.

After the groups are finished with this exercise, ask the person representing each group to describe what happened in the group for about 30-60 seconds. He or she should indicate the number of people choosing each type of dog as a first choice and last choice, and if there was any connection between the type of work a person did and his or her choice (such as if a person in sales or management chose the German Shepherd as their number one dog).

Make notes on these reports so you can look for patterns, such as the number of people whose first choice is a German Shepherd, Pomeranian, Golden Retriever, or Border Collie. Note any pattern in the last choice. You can tally the numbers as each person reports on what happened in the group. Also, note any connections between a person's work and their top choice.

Once everyone has given a report, take a minute or two to provide your feedback on the exercise. Some things to note are the following:
- Any patterns you noticed in the choices of the participants in their top dog and least favorite dog.
- Any relationship you noticed between the type of dog they chose and their type of work.

Make any other relevant comments on the exercise. Invite a few participants to share their comments or ask questions. Respond with your own comments or answers, and thank the group leaders and anyone making comments or asking questions.

Finally, take a 10-15 minute break. Invite people to network and talk about their experience in the exercise. Have coffee, water, and snacks available for the break.

CHAPTER 4: DESCRIBING THE ROOTS OF THE SYSTEM

After everyone comes back from the break, indicate that you want to briefly describe the roots of the system, and then you will have another exercise to demonstrate how effectively the Dog Type system works.

Then, provide an overview of the three major influences in creating the Dog Type system. Explain that these are the Myers-Briggs Type Indicator, the DISC Personality Profile, and the Red-Blue-Yellow-Green Color Profile System. Point out that these are time-tested personality systems that have millions of followers. The Dog Type system draws on these three systems which divide up individuals into four basic personality categories. The main points to make about each of these systems are the following:

The Myers-Briggs Type Indicator

- the Myers-Briggs Type Indicator, also known as the MBTI, dates back to 1917. It was first published in 1944 and became the Myers-Briggs Type Indicator in 1956. Eventually, it was published by the Consulting Psychologists Press in 1975, and the Center for Applications of Psychological Type (CAPT) was founded as a research laboratory on the system.
- In this system, there are 16 types based on four preferences, and you are categorized according to your choices on these four dimensions. These are whether you prefer to deal with:
    - people and things (Extraversion or "E") or ideas and information (Introversion or "I")
    - facts and reality (Sensing or "S") or possibilities and potential (Intuition or "I")
    - logic and truth (Thinking or "T") or values and relationships (Feeling or "F")
    - a well-structure lifestyle (Judgment or "J) or going with the flow (Perception or "P").
- You indicate your preference for one style over the other to get your personality type, such as ENTJ, if you are more extroverted, intuitive, thinking, and judgmental.
- To determine your type, you take a test with 93-forced choice questions which represent opposite preferences on the same dichotomy. These questions involve choosing between different word pairs or responding with a yes or no to a short statement. You get a score which indicates your preference on each of the four dichotomies, resulting in the 16 types once all of the possible choices are combined. Even if you have a certain personality type, you still use all of the styles.
- The eight types can easily be reduced to the four types that are popularized, if you drop the Thinking and Feeling category and combine Extraversion and Introversion with Sensing and Intuition.

The DISC Personality Profile

- The DISC system was born when William Moulton Marston, a graduate in the newly developing field of psychology at Harvard University, published his book *Emotions of Normal People* in 1928. According to this book, people have different styles of behavior that have developed through both internal influences and the environment, although all people share these styles in varying degrees of intensity.
- These individuals have the following characteristics, which were initially called by the first term. The second term is used now.

Dominance/Dominant (D) – direct, decisive, high ego strength, problem solver, risk taker, self-starter

Inducement/Influential (I) – enthusiastic, trusting, optimistic, persuasive, talkative, impulsive, emotional

Submission/Steady (S) – good listener, team player, possessive, steady, predictable, understanding

Compliance/Conscientious (C) – accurate, analytical, conscientious, fact-finder, systematic, high standards.

- To learn how you rate, you can take an online DISC test with 24 questions in about 10 to 15 minute.
- The DISC system has grown in popularity. It has been used by over 50 million people since 1972, especially in business, because it is less complicated and easier to understand and remember.

The Red-Blue-Yellow-Green Personality Type

- The Red-Blue-Yellow-Green Color Profile is used in various forms today, and it has been influenced by the Myers-Briggs and DISC systems.
- Two early versions of this color approach were developed by David Keirsey and Roger Birkman. Keirsey wrote a book with Marilyn Bates *Please Understand Me* in 1984 and Birkman published *True Colors* in 1995. The Birkman and Keirsey systems can be combined to show how people with different color types see the world.
- Keirsey's red "Artisans" are Birkman's red "production-centered" people, who are like the German Shepherds.
- Keirsey's yellow "Guardians" are Birkman's yellow "procedure-centered" people, who are like the Pomeranians.
- Keirsey's green "Idealists" are Birkman's green "people-centered people," who are like the Golden Retrievers.
- Keirsey's blue "Rationals" are Birkman's blue "idea-centered people," who are like Border Collies.
- These ideas are at the root of the red-yellow-green-blue color system today.
- Today, you can find all sorts of red, blue, yellow, or green personality type systems, though there are some differences in what color is associated with what traits.

Red is always the strong, dominating type, and yellow is mostly the fun, social type. But the yellows, greens, and blues vary in different versions. The basic differences, which have strong parallels with the Dog Type system, are these:

Reds are "strong leaders, fast-paced thinkers, risk takers, purpose-driven, strong-willed, and less patient. They have lots of energy, are overtly competitive, rational, and confident.

Yellows are party animals, since they are sociable, expressive, very imaginative, and enthusiastic. They are very informal, optimistic, and animated. They are relationship-focused, and have high energy.

Those with green personality traits tend to be cool, laid-back, relaxed and patient. They are easy to get along with and very informal in their approach. They are social and focus on relationships, so they can come across as emotional. They also are slower-paced in their thinking and are very democratic.

Blues are the more serious types, who are deep thinkers, analytical in nature, very detail-focused and formal in their thinking. They sometimes may seem aloof. They are deliberate in their approach and systematic, precise, and pay attention to detail. They like things in their place, and are very organized with good time management skills.

- While everyone may have a dominant personality style, everyone is a mix of all the colors.

How the Dog Type System Builds on What Has Gone Before

Sum up this discussion by explaining that the Dog Type system draws on and combines elements from these three major approaches to personality typing. Then, it adds the fun element of Dog Types, and it offers new techniques for using this system to better understand and interact with others, depending on cues you get when you talk to and observe how someone else behaves.

CHAPTER 5: ASSESSING THE DOG TYPE OF OTHERS AND LEARNING MORE ABOUT YOUR DOG TYPE

Now explain you are going to do two exercises to show participants how the Dog Types work. First, they will try to assess others' preferred type or Top Dog by mixing with others they don't know and assessing their type. Then, they will meet with others who share a similar preference and see how each group does it differently.

Assessing Another Person's Dog Type

Here's how to conduct this exercise.

Setting Up the Exercise

Explain that you will be doing an exercise in which each person has to assess another person's preferred Dog Type, and you expect to do three rounds of pairings.

Point out that you would like people to form pairs with people they don't know. Or if people know other participants, such as if they are part of an organized group or work team, ask them to pair up with the person they know the least. If there is an extra person, you can pair up with them.

Once everyone is in a pair, tell them to imagine that this is a business networking gathering and you are going around getting to know others. As such, they should in turn ask the other person a series of commonly asked questions for about 1 1/2-2 minutes each, or 3-4 minutes for each exchange. Then, they will share their perceptions of the other's Dog Type.

Adjust the time based on what seems to work best for the group. Depending on what participants, they can take turns asking and answering the questions, or one person can ask all the questions and the other person can answer, and then they should switch. As much as possible, this exchange should feel like a common conversation at a business networking gathering.

During the exchange, participants should look for cues of the other person's likely Dog Type in <u>what</u> they say about themselves and <u>how</u> they say it.

The commonly asked questions to ask are these:
- What do you do?
- What do you most like about what you do?
- How did you end up creating your business/doing your particular job?
- Where are you from?
- How did you happen to come here?
- What do you like to do for fun?

Participants can add in other questions to follow-up in response to the other person's answers, much as they might at a regular networking event. The participants can decide who should go first in asking the questions.

Let people know after 1 ½-2 minutes to let them know you are halfway through the exercise, and give them a 30 second warning to let them know the time is almost up.

Continuing the Exercise

After the 3-4 minute time is up for the first pair exchanges, ask the participants to tell each other what they think the other person's preferred Dog Type is and why they think so. Then, the other person will confirm if that's true or not. That exchange will typically take about a minute.

After that, ask the participants to find another individual to pair up with. Again the partner should be someone the person doesn't know or knows the least.

After everyone is in a pair, tell them to have a conversation like they did before.

Similarly time the exchanges. Give a 1 ½ to 2 minute warning as before, a 30-second reminder that time is almost up, nd call time at the end of the exchange. Then, ask the participants to share their assessment of the other person's Dog Type as before.

Once more, ask the participants to find another partner and participate in a 3-4 minute exchange, followed by an exchange of assessments.

Discussing the Exercise

Now take about 3 to 5 minutes to ask for comments on the exercise. Ask participants to provide the following feedback:
- How accurate were they in assessing the other person's preferred Dog Type or Top Dog?
- What cues did they look for to help them decide?
- How did they like the exercise generally?

Conclude the exercise with your observations and comments for about 3 to 5 minutes. Some of the comments you might make are the following:
- If the participants were mostly correct in making their assessments, point this out, and note that they can use this method to similarly assess the personality type of others they meet by their answers.
- If the participants had mixed results or weren't successful, ask them to share about what confused them or led them to the wrong results. Point out how this method normally results in people being very successful in making these assessments.
- Explain how participants can use this approach when they meet or talk to others to look for leads, referrals, clients, or customers or to better communicate with others to get the preferred response (such as more customers). This approach is also ideal if they have to negotiate a deal or want to create a more productive or harmonious work group.

Generally, these three exchanges, along with the time to move around and get in groups, provide feedback, and share your comments will be about 25 to 30 minutes – 15 minutes for getting into pairs and sharing, 3 to 5 minutes for feedback, and 3 to 5 minutes for your concluding comments.

Learning More about Your Dog Type

For the next exercise, ask participants to join with others who have the same Dog Type. Designate a section of the room for each of the different types. Generally, you will find that more people will be German Shepherds, Pomeranians, and Golden Retrievers, with fewer or no Border Collies. If so, you can later comment on the numbers of participants in the different groups and the relative size of the different groups.

Once people are in their groups, invite them to respond to the following questions and notice how people in their group reflect their preferred Dog Type in their responses. Explain that the articipants will generally notice commonalities with others in their group, and the idea of this exercise is to show this, although they should notice any discrepancies, too. Point out that people may be different, because they differ in their preference for their second Dog Type or Watch Dog. The questions to ask are these:
- What kind of work do you do?
- What do you most like about it?
- What do you do for fun?
- When I'm with a group of people_____ (FILL IN THE SENTENCE).
- If asked to describe myself, I would say I have these main qualities:_____.

You can tell people the questions verbally, write them on a board, or hand out a list of questions to the participants in each group. Ask people to respond to each question in turn, or for each participant to answer all of the questions in turn. Ask each group to select a reporter to report on the results to the whole group. That person can take notes or make the report from memory.

If you have any large groups, ask them to break up into smaller groups, so there are no more than 5 to 8 people in a group. For example, a group of 10 people will turn into two groups of 5 people each; a group of 12 people will become 6 people each; a group of 24 people will turn into 3 groups of 6 people each. This way, everyone should have a chance to interact and share in the group.

Then, invite the participants in each group to talk to each other about these questions for about 15-20 minutes, based on each person in the group having 2-3 minutes to answer the questions, however group members prefer to do this. Everyone can answer each question and then the group goes on to the next question; or each person can answer all of the questions in turn. Remind the participants that whoever is reporting on the group can make notes and should notice any patterns that appear in the responses of the group members.

As the groups have these discussions, you can go around to listen in on what different groups are saying, but stay in the background, so everyone can interact as if you aren't there. You don't want to interfere with the group process.

Finally, ask for a report from each group in turn. Ask the group reporter to take about 2 minutes to describe the following:
- What are the major types of work people do?
- What did people most like about their work?
- What were some of the main things people did for fun?
- What did people commonly do when in a group of people?
- What were the main qualities that people reported having?

As you listen to the reports, notice and call everyone's attention to the differences between the groups to show how the different personality types do it differently.

Thank each participant for the group report, but don't comment on it yet.

As participants give these reports, notice how these descriptions reflect the qualities of the different Dog Types. You can make notes to help you remember the main points to make after hearing the reports.

If there are several groups for a particular Dog Type, note how they are similar for each of the questions. Also, point out how the participants in different groups are different in the way they respond to these questions.

After all of the group reporters have given their reports, share your observations. In particular, note the similarities for people in the same Dog Type group and the way they differ from the members of other groups.

Finally, invite a few participants to share on the exercise and what they got out of it. In general, this exercise will take about 30 to 40 minutes, which breaks down as follows:
- 3-5 minutes for getting into groups,
- 10-15 minutes for responding to the five questions, depending on the size of the group,
- 10-15 minutes for the group reports,
- 3-5 minutes for your comments,
- 3-5 minutes for comments from a few participants about the experience.

After concluding this exercise, take another break for 10-15 minutes. Invite people to network however they want and feel free to talk about their experience in the exercise. Have coffee, water, and any snacks available for the break.

CHAPTER 6: APPLYING THE DOG TYPE SYSTEM IN YOUR BUSINESS OR WORKPLACE

Now that everyone has had a chance to understand the system and see how to use it to gain insights into the personality types of different people, show participants how to apply this system in their business or workplace. To this end, explain the strengths and weaknesses of the different types and provide examples of how participants can use this system to guide how they communicate and relate to others based on recognizing their personality type.

Indicate that participants will participate in a role-playing exercise, where they will adapt their approach based on how they assess the other person's Dog Type.

Following are guidelines for what to explain and how to conduct the exercise.

The Key Characteristics of the Four Types of Dogs

Explain that you are giving everyone a summary of the major characteristics associated with each type of dog. This will help them remember what to look for in approaching individuals with different personality types.

Print out copies of the chart for all the participants, and distribute these. Invite everyone to take a few minutes to review the chart.

DOG TYPE CHARACTERISTICS CHART

German Shepherd (Red/Dominant Type) The Leader	Pomeranian (Yellow/Influencer Type) The Fun Party Animal	Golden Retriever (Green/Steady Type) The Cool Supporter	Border Collie (Blue/Conscientious Type) The Serious Fact Checker
Strong leader	High energy, enthusiastic	Likes to help and support others	Conscientious, thorough
Has leadership skills	Expressive	Supportive	Perfectionist
Like being in control	Very animated	Interest in others	Very orderly, discipline, precise
Strong-willed	Very outgoing, sociable	Good listener	Well-organized
Wants to win, be the best	Fun loving, life of the party	Wants to cooperate, collaborate	Good time management skills
Seeks success	Often happy-go-lucky	Friendly, sociable	Likes planning, procedures
Goal-oriented	Enjoys good humor	Informal with others	Detail-oriented
Purposeful	Optimistic	Easy-going	Asks detail-oriented questions
Results-oriented	Likes good relationships	Patient	Wants accuracy, facts
Like immediate results	Relationship-focused	Normally calm, cool, collected	Logical, systematic, precise
Want to get things done	People person	Laid-back, relaxed	Uses objective reasoning
Very competitive	Likes social gatherings	Not easily upset	Analytical, deep thinker
Like challenges	Likes collaboration, collaborative	Readily adapts, adjusts	Likes coming to own conclusions
Willing to take risks, risk-taker	Loves to talk with others	Likes the familiar, comfortable	Concern with quality
Persistent	Seeks social recognition, praise, acceptance	Likes order, stability	Emphasizes competence
Optimistic	Enjoys attention, appreciation	Like keeping things organized	Wants to be right and get things right
Confident, self-assured	Most fears rejection	Good at coordinating activities	Doesn't like being wrong
Can make quick decisions, decisive	Seeks positive reinforcement	Sincere and trustworthy	Dislikes criticism
Likes getting straight to the point	Likes friendly, warm environment	Seeks sincerity, dependability	Likes to gain knowledge
Fast-paced thinker	Creates entertaining atmosphere	Values trust	Wants to show expertise
Likes facts quickly	Likes influencing/persuading	Dependable	Doesn't like small talk
Doesn't like details	Likes freedom from control		May seem aloof, reserved
Interested in big picture	Flexible		Can seem unemotional
	Doesn't like rules, procedures		Likes stability and safety
	May act impulsively		Quiet, sometimes shy
			Likes independence
			Often innovative, idea person
			Sometimes independent loners

CHAPTER 7: BETTER COMMUNICATING AND INTERACTING WITH OTHERS BASED ON THEIR DOG TYPE

Explain that participants may not know another person's Dog Type for sure, unless he or she tells them. But they can make a likely assessment based on how that person comes across, when they first meet or have an extended conversation.

To make this assessment, people should look for the following traits when they first meet or have an appointment to discuss something. Explain that the major characteristics to look for are in the chart you have given out.

Point out that the more traits a person has, the higher he or she rates in having that as a dominant personality trait, since everyone is a combination of the four types, though some types are more dominant than others. Generally, participants should look for the person's dominant type and adapt their approach to that, whether seeking a customer or client, working together or with a boss, trying to find a job, or getting to know someone in one's personal life.

Give everyone about 5 minutes to review the chart.

Adapting Your Approach to Others

Now point out how participants can use the personality, behaviors, and interests of the different Dog Types to help them vary their approach to sales, working together, managing or coordinating a team, seeking a job, or having better relationships in their personal life.

Take about 20 minutes to describe how participants can adapt their approach, using examples from different situations. Then, participants will do role plays with individuals representing different types.

Here are some highlights to point out about each type.

Relating to the German Shepherd (Red/Dominant Leadership Type)
- Very bottom-line, results oriented
- Wants the big picture
- Very interested in winning, success, getting to goals, and getting things done.
- While you want to include some facts to support your point of view, make your presentation or meeting brief and to the point.
    - Don't spend much time socializing or making small talk.
    - Quickly emphasize the benefits.
    - Don't get bogged down presenting the features or why something works.
    - A few examples might be enough to support your point of view.
- Since the German-Shepherd type sees him or herself as a leader, defer to his or her lead, should he or she ask any questions or ask for more information.

- If you offer supporting handouts or reports, include a short executive-type summary or abstract to highlights the main points. Perhaps include a few graphs, photos, and illustrations to make the point even more dramatically.
- Emphasize how the person can win and succeed with whatever you are offering.
- Mention any challenges or risks, but emphasize how one can overcome them and receive recognition for succeeding. Point out that success is likely, since you believe the person has the skills to make this happen, and show how you can help him or her win.
- Emphasize the recognition and prestige from doing what you propose.
- Position yourself as a subordinate or right hand person who is there to help, not as a co-leader which could challenge the German Shepherds desire to be the leader.

Relating to the Pomeranian (Yellow/Influencer/Fun Party Animal Type)
- Very social, loves to collaborate and work with others
- Loves attention and appreciation
- Very high energy, happy-go-lucky
- Very outgoing, and likes fun, fun, fun
- Take some time to get to know the Pomeranian and engage in small talk.
- Show you have common interests, know some of the same people, and go to some of the same places.
- Start off by developing some rapport and then make your presentation.
- Be friendly and share a joke or two if appropriate.
- Listen attentively with a big smile, since the Pomeranian loves to talk.
- Try to match the Pomeranian's high energy, enthusiastic style.
- Smile and gesture a lot.
- Be warm and show how you want to work together like a collaborator in a fun project all involved will enjoy.

Relating to the Golden Retriever (Green/Steady/Cool Supporter)
- Very friendly, sociable, cooperative, and supportive
- Tends to be informal
- Likes order, stability, and keeping things organized
- Be casual and sociable.
- Take a little time to be social and show how you like working with others.
- Point out how what you are doing is designed to help others and is a well-organized program.
- Since the Golden Retriever type likes things to be calm and steady, be cool and collected in your presentation.

Relating to the Border Collie (Blue/Conscientious/the Serious Fact Checker)
- Tends to be more serious and reserved
- Often introverts who like being by themselves and working independently
- Concerned with facts and details
- Point up the evidence for why this program works or provides value.
- Emphasize the quality of whatever you are offering

- Highlight the competence and knowledge that has gone into creating the program and the experience of those involved.
- Don't spend time with small talk or socializing.
- Highlight the facts.
- Point out your own expertise and that of anyone involved in the project.
- Mention any degrees or other credentials.
- If the person asks probing questions, be prepared to answer them.
- If appropriate, provide more details later, or if convenient, give the person the supporting materials now.

Summing Up

Sum up the overview of different Dog Types and how to approach them by emphasizing how knowing this information can help them better communicate with and relate to others in a wide variety of situations – from sales to working with others to managing people to finding new clients or a job.

Explain that you will give a few examples of use this knowledge in different situations, and then everyone will participate in a role play.

Some Examples of Using the Dog Type System in Different Situations

Give a few examples of how the Dog Type system works. Use the examples that relate to the individuals participating in this workshop.

Making a Sale of a Product or Service

Explain that in a regular sales presentation, you have to do some basic preparation in order to effectively approach any prospective customer or client to make a sale. Then, you adapt what you say based on the person's personality type, when you follow-up after a networking meeting, make an initial sales call to set up a meeting, or talk to the person on the phone. If you don't have any advance information about the person, seek cues from your initial encounter in the person's speaking style, body language, or type of business.

For example, if you are making a pitch to a company with a bottom line orientation, such as a bank, you would act like you are making a presentation to a German Shepherd. On the other hand, if you are making a pitch to an organization with a fun reputation, such as a nightclub or hip new coffee house, you might treat the person you deal with like a Pomeranian and highlight how your product or service will add to everyone's fun. Or suppose you speak with someone from a service organization, non-profit, or health club. You might start off like you were making a pitch to a Golden Retriever and emphasize how your product or service will help people better work together cooperatively. If you are meeting with someone in the tech field, you might begin as if you are dealing with a Border Collie. Since they like facts and details, you might start off by pointing out the success your product or service has gained, the number of users it has, and how much sales have been growing because people like the product or service.

Looking for Clients or Referrals at a Networking Event

Note that at a networking event, a primary goal is to meet many people, exchange business cards with people, and plan to follow-up later. The goal is to focus on getting new business and quickly determining who might be a promising lead or referral partner.

So talk about the importance of the 15-30 second elevator speech, and how people can adapt that to their perception of the other person's personality type.

Point out that good way to start is by asking the other person what he or she does. This way, by getting the other person talking first, you can not only find out about the business but learn more about the other person's personality type. So don't only look for what the person says, but how he or she says it.

For example, if the person is very direct, concise, and confident, that's a sign of the German Shepherd. If he or she is very high-energy, upbeat, and sociable, that suggests the Pomeranian. If he or she is more casual and laid back, that might be a Golden Retriever. Finally, if he or she seems quiet and provides a detailed description of a product, service, or company, that's the sign of a Border Collie.

Also suggest that people might combine an awareness of what the person says with signifiers from the person's appearance. For instance, a conservative suit with a power tie for a man and a stylish suit with subdued jewelry for a woman are signs of a German Shepherd. But if you see anything flashy, such as a color tie for a man, shiny and uniquely styled jewelry for the woman, those suggest the Pomeranian. If the person is dressed more informally or casually, that suggests the Golden Retriever. If the person's dress is even more informal, out of style, or geeky, that could point to the Border Collie.

What if the other person asks about you first? Suggest that participants start with their standard elevator speech, where they highlight the benefits and quickly state what they do, since networking events favor the German Shepherd style of quickly getting to the point about the benefits you provide and what you do. Then, when the other person shares, notice personality signs for the different Dog Types. Use those for your follow-up when you call or email to set up a further meeting. Later, as you improve your assessment of a person's Dog Type, you can adapt your style accordingly, depending on whether you are primarily dealing with a German Shepherd, Pomeranian, Golden Retriever, or Border Collie.

Improving Your Relationships with Co-Workers, Your Boss, or Your Employees in the Workplace

If the workshop participants are interested in improving workplace relationships, use examples to show how the Dog Type system can help with better relationships, since individuals can better know how to communicate or interact with someone. The result can be better teams, better decisions about giving assignments to people with different skills and sensibilities, and a better ability to resolve conflicts.

You can use the following examples to illustrate how the system might work in the workplace, depending on what participants are most interested in, such as better relationships with co-workers, with their boss, or in managing employees. Some examples are the following:

- **Relating to the German Shepherd**
  - If your co-worker or boss is like a German Shepherd, you can be more direct and to the point in what you say, and they will be particularly interested in anything that makes the work more productive. Your co-worker may like to know about becoming more productive, too, because it can help to do things more efficiently and effectively, which will impress the boss. Your boss may be especially impressed, since that will mean the company, team, or department will be more productive, resulting in more profits.
  - Suppose a boss has an employee who is like a German Shepherd. This might be a good person to put in charge of a team or given more responsibility. If the boss wants the person to do something, he or she can explain the directions more succinctly and directly. The boss might emphasize that this change is to make operations go more smoothly, resulting in more productivity and profits for the company – and perhaps more bonuses and incentives for employees.

- **Relating to the Pomeranian**
  - What if your co-worker or boss is more like a Pomeranian? Then, talk with lots of energy and enthusiasm, and if the co-worker or boss wants, take some time to socialize together.
  - Should you be a boss and you feel an employee is like a Pomeranian, consider that in giving out work assignments. Maybe the Pomeranian would be more suited to be a receptionist, answering phones, or moving into sales. Or you might engage in some social chatter to help the Pomeranian feel more comfortable and at home on the job, since Pomeranians love to be friendly and sociable.

- **Relating to the Golden Retriever**
  - Say your co-worker or boss is more like a Golden Retriever, which means they like helping and supporting others; they hope everyone will work well together and get along. In this case, it helps to show you are a good team player too. Indicate that you want to cooperate with the group and go along with what the group decides. If you make suggestions, emphasize how a proposed change will contribute to employee morale and satisfaction. While the change might benefit productivity, profits, and the bottom line, stress how any changes will be a win-win for everyone. Or perhaps suggest activities to help others, such as organizing a birthday party for a colleague or getting contributions for a gift for an employee who has had a family emergency.

- Or say you are a boss and an employee acts like a Golden Retriever. In that case, you might praise the employee for the ways he or she contributes to the morale and satisfaction of other employees. Perhaps invite the employee to help you or a team leader organize an office party, or invite the employee to be part of a welcome committee to orient new employees.

- **<u>Relating to the Border Collie</u>**
    - What if a co-worker or boss is more like a Border Collie? Then, you want to share facts and details with them. For example, if you are working with a Border Collie on a project, you might focus on doing the work with little conversation, since Border Collies like doing something carefully and accurately, and they prefer not to have distractions.
    - If you are a boss with a Border Collie employee, find things that the employee has done right to praise, because Border Collies like to be recognized for their skills and abilities and like to be known for doing things well. Also, where appropriate, let the employee do things independently or in their own way, so they get the best results, since Border Collie types are often loners, so they do well working on their own. You might also invite the Border Collies to do reports on how a work group is doing or review and proof any reports that others do for accuracy, since Border Collies are good at detailed, analytical work.

<u>Getting a Job or Promotion</u>

Finally, if attendees are looking for a job or promotion, use examples of job seekers succeeding in their search to show how the Dog Type system can help them. Point out the importance of considering the type of person doing the hiring or promotion or leading the committee which is making these decisions. They can also consider the company's culture, which one can learn about on its website.

Some things to point out for job seekers are these:

- If you have been working with a boss, you generally already know what he or she is like when you are up for a promotion or seeking a reassignment, so adapt your approach for more or different responsibility accordingly.
- If you don't know much if anything about the new boss doing the hiring, take into consideration the type of company and what you can learn about the company's culture, since companies hope for a good fit with new hires. For example, if you are seeking a job in law or finance, the leadership will typically be German Shepherd types. If you are interested in sales or sales management, you are likely to meet a mix of German Shepherds and Pomeranians. Should you be looking at non-profit organizations, government agencies, or health clubs, you are likely to encounter a lot of Golden Retrievers. And if you are approaching a company involved in high-tech, research, or planning, you are likely to find a lot of Border Collies, who are very detail and fact-oriented.

- If you aren't sure how to adapt your job pitch, imagine that you are doing your pitch to a German Shepherd type, where you briefly highlight the benefits you bring to the job and why you are qualified to provide these benefits. You might point up how you are very fast and productive in whatever you do, and if you have testimonials or references, mention them. You can always adapt your pitch as you go along, if you sense the employer is a different type.

- If you feel the boss or hiring committee are Pomeranian types, show more enthusiasm and energy when you pitch yourself and your credentials. Briefly start off with some comments to build rapport, such as enthusiastically stating how much you appreciate what the company is doing and how you can easily fit in with the group.

- If you feel you are pitching to Golden Retriever types, be calm, cool, and collected as you speak about what you bring to the table. Emphasize how you can be a good team player and support others in the company. If the organization is supporting any causes or charities, describe how you appreciate their contribution and hope that you can contribute, too.

- If you meet with a Border Collie type, be ready to support what you say about yourself with facts and details. Offer to show examples of work you have done. If you have a list of references or testimonials, hand them over. In this way, you not only show supporting evidence about what you have done, but you show you are a person who likes the facts and details, too.

Conducting a Roleplay on Adapting Your Approach to Different Dog Types

After explaining how to adapt a presentation to different types, guide participants in a role play. Use a scenario based on the main interest of the workshop participants (i.e.: selling of a product or service, looking for clients or referral partners at networking event, improving relationships at work, or finding a job). Whatever the focus of the scenario, the basic format of the roleplay will be the same.

Ask people to form into pairs, preferably with someone they don't know or don't know very well. Explain that they will be switching roles with one person being the presenter and the other person the responder. The responder will be a customer, potential client, co-worker, boss, employee, or job interviewer, depending on the main interest of the workshop participants.

Once participants have formed into pairs ask them to choose who goes first. Then, give them these instructions.

Tell the presenter he will be doing a pitch for one of the following purposes, based on the focus of the presentation:
- sell a product or service of his or her choice
- interest the other person in being a potential client or referral partner, and set up a phone call or meeting to discuss this possibility further
- improve a relationship between co-workers, with your boss, or with an employee
- change a program, work assignment, or other activities at work

- get a job or work assignment.

Finally, announce the responder's personality type – whether a German Shepherd, Pomeranian, Golden Retriever, or Border Collie. You can use the standard order in which these personality types are normally presented, or mix them up by drawing one of the cards. A form you can cut up for this purpose is on the following page. Just mix up the four cards and draw one for each round of these exchanges.

After you announce the responder's personality type, the presenter will make the presentation and the responder will listen and respond, as if this is a real presentation to someone with that personality type.

Give each presenter 3 minutes to make their pitch and have a conversation with the responder.

Next, ask the pairs to switch roles, so the presenter becomes the responder and the responder becomes the presenter.

Again, give the pairs 3 minutes for the exchange.

Then, ask the participants to find a new partner for the next presentation. Once everyone is paired up again, ask them to decide between them who will go first as the presenter and responder.

Now announce the responder's Dog Type, and the presenter will have 3 minutes to make the presentation and the responder can respond as this different Dog Type.

At the end of 3 minutes, ask the participants to switch roles. Now the responder will become the presenter and the responder will be the presenter as before.

For the third time, give the same instructions and assign the responder the third Dog Type role. Again, give the pairs 3 minutes for each role.

Finally, for the fourth time, give the same instructions and assign the responder the fourth Dog Type role. Again, give the pairs 3 minutes for each role.

After the pairs have experienced being presenters and responders in all four roles, tell the participants they will now discuss the experience and share what they learned. So they should get in groups with two pairs or 4 people each. If there is an odd pair, they should join one of the other groups, so there will be 6 people in that group.

Then, in these groups of pairs, ask them to discuss the following questions for about 5 to 7 minutes. You can review the questions on a PowerPoint slide or write them on a board to help participants remember them. Ask the groups to choose a member to report back to everyone. That person can write down notes during the discussion to help remember the highlights, if he or she wishes. The questions to discuss are:

- What was your experience in the exercise?
- What did you notice about the differences in the presentations to the different Dog Types?
- How comfortable were you with different types of presentations?
- How did the responders react differently when they were different Dog Types?
- Are there any other observations about the exercise?

As the groups share, go around and listen in to the groups without interrupting them. Notice how the different discussions are going and if there are common themes in different groups.

Let participants know when there is about a minute left, so they can wrap up their discussion.

Then, ask the reporter for each group to describe the main comments and issues that came up during the discussion. Allow each reporter about 1-2 minutes for this report.

After someone has reported for every group, share your observations and comments about the major topics that came up. Note how the exercise illustrates the differences in how to approach individuals with different personality types.

THE FOUR DOG TYPE CARDS

Use the following cards to randomize the order in which you announce the different Dog Types when individuals are acting as presenters and respondents in pairs.

GERMAN SHEPHERD	**POMERANIAN**
GOLDEN RETRIEVER	**BORDER COLLIE**

CHAPTER 8: QUICKLY IDENTIFYING THE DIFFERENT DOG TYPES

Explain that you will now provide participants with a good way to quickly identify the types of individuals who are likely to have different personality types. Indicate that you will give everyone a chart that indicates where they might be likely to meet the different types and some of their characteristics.

Like other charts you have given them, they can use this chart as a quick guide to imagining what a person will be like before they meet. Then, they can modify their initial impression based on what they learn about the other person. Remind everyone that different people will have differing degrees of strength in their most dominant and next dominant traits, and some people may not to fit the usual personality profile for a particular occupation.

Point out that participants can put themselves on the chart by numbering the categories according to their first (Top Dog), second (Watch Dog), third (Sleuth Dog), and fourth (Underdog) type. Note that in some systems, their third ranked trait is referred to as your "secret weapon," or here your (Sleuth Dog), because under certain situations that third ranked type can be a hidden strength, as in the example of a real estate agent described in *Using the Dog Type System for Success in Business and the Workplace*.

Also note that the chart can be used to illustrate how the different types might work well together, if one is looking for a partner or employees. For example, a hard-driving German Shepherd may find a Golden Retriever provides a good balance by providing the warmth and support a prospective client needs to enter into an agreement. Or a Pomeranian might find the perfect employee in a Border Collie, since the Pomeranian can be a great promoter, while the Border Collie takes care of the details and follow-up.

Suggest that participants can think of how other combos can work well together. Print and hand out copies of the chart to participants. Invite them to discuss their type and how they might work with other types, based on major similarities and differences, such as whether a person is more task or people oriented, a faster or slower thinker, and more guided by their heart/emotions or their brain/reasons.

DOG TYPE OCCUPATIONS AND THINKING AND EMOTIONAL ORIENTATIONS

	Faster Thinking and Decision-Making	
Task-Brain Oriented	**German Shepherd (Leader/Red)** Type of Occupations: Politician, Manager, VP, Sales Rep, CEO	**Pomeranian (Promoter/Yellow)** Types of Occupations: Sales, Marketing Publicity, Speaker, Tour Guide, Campaign Manager, Entertainment, Social Media Guru, Event Planners
	Border Collie (Researcher/Blue) Type of Occupations: Scientist, Engineer, Academic, Professor, Researcher, CPA, Accountant, IT Professional, Computer Programmer	**Golden Retriever (Supporter/Green)** Type of Occupations: Social Worker, Therapist, Senior Care, Massage, Health Practitioner, Coaches, Non-Profit Employee, Hospitality Support Staff, Arts, Activists, Volunteers	**People-Heart Oriented**
	Slower Thinking and Decision-Making	

Using the Dog Type Occupations and Orientations Chart

Finally, ask participants to use their rankings to draw a Circle of Strength in the center of the chart to indicate their relative strength in each area. (Or they can use a Star of Strength with four points, where the position or the size of the points reflects the rating.)

Explain how the strength of the different ratings is used to position the circle or star points to graphically show a person's relative strengths in each area. Use the Circle of Strength and Star of Strength Charts on the following page as an example.

Print and pass out the charts, which show how a circle or star can be positioned around the center of the chart to show the relative strength of each type. In the example, the Circle or Star of Strength are based on the following ratings:

German Shepherd (Top Dog) – 9
Border Collie (Watch Dog) – 8
Pomeranian (Sleuth Dog) - 4
Golden Retriever (Underdog) – 3

Tell participants to take their own ratings on a scale of 1-10 for each type of Dog (either done previously or done now) and put that number in the quadrant for that Dog Type. Then, they should draw and position a circle to reflect their relative strength in each area. If there is a tie, they should break it by assigning one of the pair a higher or lower number. Give participants about 5 minutes to do this.

After participants draw their circles or stars on their charts, lead a discussion of how the chart shows their traits. Point out that they can similarly estimate where someone else might fall in these four quadrants and draw a profile for them to help deciding how to relate to that person.

CIRCLE OF STRENGTH AND STAR OF STRENGTH CHARTS

Circle of Strength

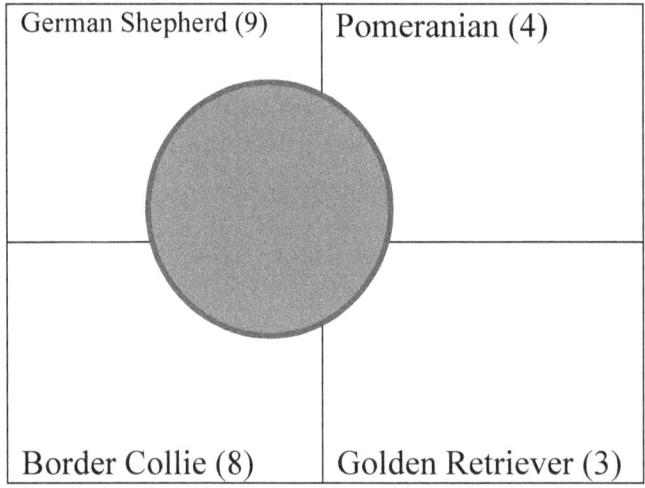

Star of Strength

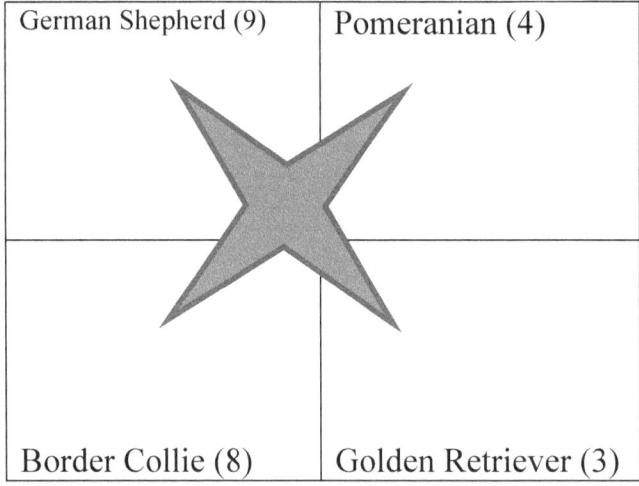

CREATING YOUR OWN CIRCLE OR STAR OF STRENGTH

Enter how you rate yourself for each type from 1-10. Then, draw a circle or star on the chart to reflect the relative strength of each of the types.

Circle of Strength

German Shepherd ( )	Pomeranian ( )
Border Collie ( )	Golden Retriever ( )

Star of Strength

German Shepherd ( )	Pomeranian ( )
Border Collie ( )	Golden Retriever ( )

CHAPTER 9: WRAPPING UP THE WORKSHOP

To wrap up the workshop, ask everyone to return to their original seats.

Summary of the Workshop

Briefly summarize the main things you did during the workshop:
- Introduced the different Dog Types
- Described how the Dog Type system developed
- Had people determine their primary Dog Type
- Showed how to assess someone else's Dog Type
- Led an exercise to demonstrate one's ability to assess someone else's Dog Type
- Led an exercise where people got together with others of their Dog Type
- Discussed how people could use the Dog Types to be more effective in different situations, including sales, finding prospects at networking events, improving relationships at work, and finding a job
- Led an exercise on doing presentations to people with different Dog Types.

Evaluating the Workshop

Ask people to share their experience of the workshop and what they gained from it. Call on 4 to 6 people to share their comments.

Explain that you will be handing out evaluation forms for everyone to fill out, and you would like feedback on what people liked and what they would change or improve. Also, indicate that you will giving a prize to those who complete and turn in the evaluation form. If people don't want to include their name, they can list their Dog Type and make up a Dog Name.

Show the prizes you are offering. These might include a bottle of wine, *The Dog Type System for Success in Business or the Workplace,* a coupon for a free or reduced price follow-up program, or a combination of offerings. Select prizes which will be desirable for this group.

Let people know they will have about 5 minutes to finish the Evaluation Forms and turn them in. They must be present to win.

Now distribute the forms. A copy of a form you can print is at the end of this chapter.

Ask people to pass their forms to the front or have some helpers collect them.

Glance through the forms as people turn them in, fold those that are complete into quarters, and put them in a bowl. Mix up the forms, and ask a helper or volunteer to pick the prize winner by selecting an Evaluation Form without looking. Then, announce the name of the winner and award the prize.

DOG TYPE EVALUATION QUESTIONNAIRE

1. How would you rate your experience of the workshop on a scale of 0-10? _____

2. What did you most like about today's workshop and why?

3. What did you least like or think could be changed or improved and why?

4. Do you have any recommendations for companies or organizations that might benefit from this workshop? If so, list them and include any contact information.

5. If you liked this program, can you include your comments or a testimonial which we can quote with your name? If so, include your name, company, title, city, and state. We can include your website if you like.

6. Would you like to be involved in any future programs, and how would you like to contribute? If so, include your name, email and phone number.

7. Would you like to be on our mailing list to receive our newsletter or information about future programs that may be of interest to you? If so, check yes. If you haven't already listed your name and email, please include it below.

    Yes: _____

    Name:_____   Email:_____

Final Comments

To conclude the workshop, express how much you enjoyed being with the group.

Describe any plans you have for the future, such as future workshops, books, videos, and courses. Indicate if you or the Dog Type Association (DTA) have any programs scheduled and where these will be.

Ask people to refer any individuals or organizations who might be interested in you presenting a workshop for their group.

Ask anyone with a relevant announcement for the group to make it.

Thank anyone who helped you put on the program and make it a success.

Invite people to stay around and network for the next 15 to 20 minutes, while you put everything away and clean up the room.

Then, mix and mingle with the attendees for about 5 to 10 minutes. After that, clean up with the help of any helpers and set up the room as requested by the facility hosting the workshop.

What's Next

We have many ideas for building the Dog Types system, and we invite those interested in joining our network and giving workshops to let us know now or by email.

We will soon have a parallel system based on Cat Type for the millions of people who love cats. As with the Dog Types system, people can identify most closely with four types of cats, such as a Savannah or Bengal Cat, which is tough like a German Shepherd, or the Ragdoll Cat, which is fun and friendly like the Pomeranian.

As you prefer, you can use your Dog or Cat Type profile or both. The systems and methods are the same, except one will feature dogs and the other will use cats.

Now that you know the system and how to apply it, start using it to have more success in your business and at work. And let us know the results. As German Shepherds and Border Collies ourselves, we'd really like to know.

ABOUT THE AUTHOR

GINI GRAHAM SCOTT, Ph.D., J.D., is a nationally known writer, consultant, speaker, and seminar leader, specializing in social trends, popular culture, business and work relationships, and professional and personal development. She has published over 50 books on diverse subjects with major publishers. She has worked with dozens of clients on memoirs, self-help, and popular business books, as well as film scripts. Her websites include www.changemakerspublishingandwriting.com and www.ginigrahamscott.com. She is a Huffington Post regular columnist, commenting on social trends, new technology, business, and everyday life at www.huffingtonpost.com/gini-graham-scott.

She is the founder of Changemakers Publishing featuring books on social trends, work, business, psychology, and self-help, which has published over 100 Print, e-books, and audiobooks. She has licensed several dozen books for foreign sales, including in the UK, Russia, Korea, Spain, Indonesia, and Japan.

She has written numerous books on creativity and visualization, including *Mind Power: Picture Your Way to Success; The Empowered Mind: How to Harness the Creative Force within You;* and *Want It, See It, Get It!*

She has received national media exposure for her books, including appearances on *Good Morning America, Oprah,* and *CNN*. She has been the producer and host of a talk show series, CHANGEMAKERS, featuring interviews on social trends.

Scott is active in a number of community and business groups, including the Lafayette, Danville, and Pleasant Hill Chambers of Commerce. She is a graduate of the prestigious Leadership in Contra Costa County program and is a member of a BNI group in Walnut Creek, B2B groups in Danville and Walnut Creek, and many other business networking groups. She is the organizer of six Meetup groups in the film and publishing industries with over 6000 members in Los Angeles and the San Francisco Bay Area. She also does workshops and seminars on the topics of her books.

She received her Ph.D. from the University of California, Berkeley, and her J.D. from the University of San Francisco Law School. She has received five MAs at Cal State, East Bay, including most recently an MA in Communications. She will be starting an additional MA program in history there in the fall of 2017.

CHANGEMAKERS PUBLISHING
3527 Mt. Diablo Blvd., #273
Lafayette, CA 94549
changemakers@pacbell.net . (925) 385-0608
www.changemakerspublishingandwriting.com

www.ingramcontent.com/pod-product-compliance
Lightning Source LLC
Chambersburg PA
CBHW081204020426
42333CB00020B/2616